# GUMBO JOY

## BY ROBERT P. DIXON JR.

All inquiries or sales request should be addressed to:

Planting People Growing Justice Press
P.O. Box 131894
Saint Paul, MN 55113
www.ppgjli.org

Printed and bound in the United States of America
First Edition
LCCN: 2021952436
SC ISBN: 978-1-7351239-2-9

I dedicate this book to my daughter (Nylah), my Dad (Bob D.), my Mom (Sylvia), my sister (Anita), my brother (Bryan), my brother (Enrique), my sister (Lisa), and my entire family.

I also wish to dedicate this book to all the girl dads and real dads who love and cherish all children even those that are not theirs.

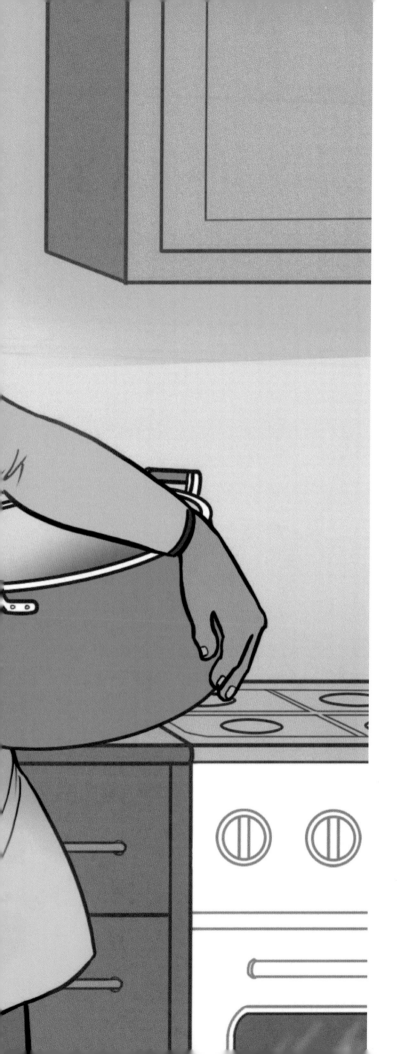

Every Sunday, Papa and Rose make a pot of joy.

Rose brings Papa one big blue pot.

Papa places the pot on the stove.

Papa reminds Rose that gumbo represents **two** cultures coming together, from West Africa's shores to New Orleans, Louisiana. This is beaucoup, a French word for many cultures.

The name gumbo comes from the word okra.

Rose gathers
**three** hands full of
vegetables.

Crisp celery, brightly
colored bell peppers.

Papa helps by bringing
the onions, garlic and
shallots.

Papa opens **four** packages from the French Market in the Quarters.

1 big package of fresh shrimp

1 filled with Andouille Sausage

1 big bag of fresh crabs

1 package of chicken wings and legs

Papa is stirring the roux in the pot.

Rose counts up to five for each time Papa stirs the spoon in the pot.

1 swirl, 2 swirls, 3 swirls, 4 swirls, 5 swirls

Papa chops **six** bowls of vegetables.

Rose helps Papa add the vegetables in the big blue pot.

Papa adds seven bowls of Andouille Sausage along with the chicken into the pot.

Rose watches very intently so she can learn how to cook gumbo like Papa.

**Eight** family members rush into the kitchen: PawPaw, MawMaw, Auntie, Uncle and four cousins.

MawMaw greets everyone with a hug, gentle kiss and a solemn reminder to "wash their hands when entering her kitchen."

The kitchen is filled with laughter and dancing.

Rose claps nine beats to the second line song.

The gumbo simmers and fills the air with the scent of joy.

Rose prepares the table with **ten** bowls for the entire family.

Papa reminds Rose: "Gumbo is the smell of love."

Rose smiles with joy.

# History of Gumbo

Gumbo represents beaucoup. This is a French word for many, reflecting the many cultures represented in each bowl of gumbo.

Gumbo's origin is from West Africa to Spain to France to New Orleans, Louisiana.

The name Gumbo comes from the West African central Bantu dialect. The word for okra is "ki ngombo," or, in its shortened form, gombo.

(Image by Lara Hata, canva.com)

# About the Author

Robert P. Dixon Jr. is a proud New Orleans native.

He learned these key aspects about cooking gumbo by going to all his neighborhood friends' homes in one day. He would eat at every person's house he stopped at.

This was his routine after school and on the weekends. Once he finished his routine, he'd still eat once he got home. He joined every bowl of "gumbo joy." You can join the joy too. Bon appétit!

PLANTING PEOPLE
GROWING JUSTICE

Planting People Growing Justice Leadership Institute seeks to plant seeds of social change through education, training, and community outreach.

A portion of the proceeds from the sale of this book will support the educational programming of Planting People Growing Justice Leadership Institute.

Learn more at www.ppgjli.org

Made in the USA
Coppell, TX
07 April 2022

76144669R00019